THOUGHT CATALOG BOOKS

Eternal Youth

Eternal Youth

A Collection of Poetry

MARIA ELENA

Thought Catalog Books

Brooklyn, NY

THOUGHT CATALOG BOOKS

For us,

and those who made us feel something.

Contents

Introduction

I remember the moment I fell in love with poetry. It was a cloudy day in elementary school and I was wearing my pastel blue tracksuit. That entire year I refused to wear anything but sweatpants because "jeans made my legs feel frozen." In my free time, I was constantly rereading *Chamber of Secrets*, playing with Neopets all night while my parents were asleep, and writing my own stories. Naturally, when my English teacher saw these stories, she sat me down privately and told me I have a gift for writing. This is something I probably wouldn't have noticed if she didn't bring it up to me. I mean, come on! I was eight years old, and all I cared about was getting home so I could watch cartoons and eat my weight in artificially-flavored cheese snacks. (Ironically, this is still all I care about.) So when that same teacher introduced me and the rest of my class to poetry, you can pretty much guess what happened.

I started out writing poems about how much I wanted to try Kronk's spinach puffs from *The Emperor's New Groove*, all of the adventures my teddy bear Grumpy and I went on, and asking questions such as, "Why is the sky blue? Why do cows say 'moo?' Why, oh why, do I love you?"

Things have changed since then. In middle school I wrote mostly about my emo, short-lived relationships and how difficult my (very easy) life was. In high school I wrote about falling in love for the first time, dealing with mental health issues, and dreaming of a better life in an almost transcendental way. Now, I write about everything from my experience being a woman in the twenty-first century, to how much capitalism sucks, all the way to finding your place in the universe.

When I found out Eternal Youth was going to be published, 95% of it was already written. All I had to do was consolidate my poems, edit them, and ultimately figure out which ones were worthy of actually being published.

However, poetry has changed. Hell, the English language has even changed. Why was I putting so much pressure on myself to be like Plath or Dickinson or Angelou? I'm Maria Elena, not some Plath-Dickinson-Angelou hybrid!

Poetry (for Millennials, at least) has become more of a general commentary on universally relatable topics instead of an entire personal poem. Basically, poetry nowadays is less about pouring your soul onto the paper and more about what looks more aesthetically pleasing. It's all about minimalism. A few pretty sentences with pretty words with a pretty illustration that you'd reblog on Tumblr or post on Instagram. When you read it, you relate to it…but you don't really feel it. The poem has no distinct voice and it doesn't really tell a story…it describes a brief situation or feeling. However, it's pretty and simple. People like that. Who would want to read poetry that confuses them? That they can't 100% relate to? That's too long? That just reads as an entire mess?

Let's just face the facts here: not everyone wants to read Shakespearean sonnets and ancient epics anymore. (However, if you do, we should *definitely* get coffee sometime.)

During the process of putting together *Eternal Youth*, I was torn between comparing myself to these legendary poets and wanting to sell out to the 'minimalistic' trend. Until, of course, I realized the root of my mini-crisis: seeking validation. If I purposely set myself apart from all other modern poets, I would be getting validation from older souls and those who live and breathe poetry. Maybe I would be noticed by prestigious literary journals…and if I was lucky, *The New Yorker*.

And if I were to conform to this modern "minimalistic" trend, I would be getting validation from my fellow Millennials and those who live and breathe the Internet. Maybe I would be noticed by prestigious women's lifestyle magazines…and if I was lucky, *Teen Vogue*.

Both forms of validation wouldn't even truly satisfy me considering I would be altering myself, my stories and my poetry. This completely goes against my belief that poetry is rooted in authentic emotion and created by the uncontrollable urge to write. As William Wordsworth said, "Poetry is the spontaneous overflow of powerful feelings: it takes its origin from emotion recollected in tranquility." The best thing any artist can do is to put out art that reflects who they truly are. And that's what I decided to do.

Everything you're about to read is *allllll* me. It's written with love, and now that I mention it, 1,714 other emotions. I'm complex and I'm messy, so I can't expect my poetry to be any different. These words were written over the course of a decade. In autumns, winters, summers and springs. The West Coast, the East Coast, the Midwest. Different areas, different feelings, and different reading levels. Some are quite immature and embarrassing. Some of them I love so much I would tattoo the words on my forehead.

Regardless, all of these poems were written by me at some point in my youth and I refuse to censor that. These words are a representation of my heart, my soul….and my eternal youth. I hope you like it.

Welcome to Eternal Youth. Sit back, grab a bag of hot Cheetos, and enjoy my vulnerability.

Maria Elena

The Virgin and the Ram

They will not remember me
They will not remember you
They will remember us

Lonely tourists will stand and stare
Harlequin hearts beating across the Atlantic
Surrounded by blue roses and tall buildings
The flashing lights blurring out the decaying cadavers

The ocean envies the depth of our love
The angels, the demons will take us

Transparency

Introverted thoughts running through my brain
Observing limpid smiles and words that make me cringe

Flipping through a thesaurus looking for synonyms of yourself
Uncertainty clogs your mind, flushes it out with small talk

You sit in the back begging for approval
Feeding off the laughter of acquaintances to mend your paper heart

Eraser marks and scribbles fill a page that isn't even yours
Rip out a new page and make it your own

Your image projects on a whiteboard for everyone to see
I see right through you like a transparency

Love and Art

I will always cherish your musky smell, your soft skin and the way
your lips linger on mine at the end of every kiss

Your eyes convey more emotion than words or pictures
And I love you

I will not search anymore
My star-crossed soul is at peace

Heaven became reality
Reality became fantasy
It's always been you

You are my purpose, my passion
The beginning and end of every thought
My first, my last, my love eternal

If you are the paintbrush, then I am the paint
Together we are a masterpiece
Our love is a work of art

1952

I walk into an empty room,
trying to remember what was here before me.
I vaguely remember the faded yellow walls and the lavender sheets.
Feeling numb, nothing left but dreamy nihilism and nostalgia for a
time I never knew.
Living life in solitude isn't too bad when I'm with you.
Dressed in pastel chiffon and flower crowns,
You're in your studded boots and black button down.
Corner cafés, spiral staircases, and Polaroid pictures.
Sharing vanilla milkshakes and listening to Frank Sinatra records.
Take me to the theatre, give me a suburban escape.
I'll wear a pink Chanel suit and pearls.
My bones were decaying, my mind was dying.
I found a light that never goes out in your narrow eyes.
The American dream made me come alive.
Make your life a work of art and you will never die.

Snowflakes

Heavy eyelids and demonic hallucinations,
drifting away into nothing.
Going, going…gone.

The drowning sound of static awakens me just before dawn.
I do not move.
I am enjoying the darkness, I am enjoying the silence.

Moments pass.
The night is dead, the sun has risen.
Caffeinated thoughts and synthetic yawns.

Time is ticking.
Growing older with mindless bodies in a concrete box.
Same time, same place, same feeling.

The seasons change.
Unfortunately I cannot embrace spring's blooming flowers.
I cannot feel the comfort of summer's warm touch,
nor can I appreciate the beauty of autumn and its colors.

The snowflakes will fall,
I will stay standing.

Ecstasy

Loving him is cinnamon tea,
autumn lullabies and oak trees.

Baby voice, porcelain skin.
Black dress, long hair, cupcake grin.

I'm your little baby princess, your schoolgirl crush.
I'm your candy-coated mess, your sweetheart lush.

Hold my hand in front of the pearly gates,
our infinite paradise now awaits.

Californian Conversations

I wish I could fall asleep with the stars.
Oh, what I'd give to see how brightly they shine.

I'd love to wake up to complete silence, white sheets, and the smell
of crisp air and roses.

I'd love to swim the depths of the ocean with the mermaids and
prance around windy meadows with the fairies.

No one around for miles, nothing to pollute my pure white soul.
Just nature and me.

Twin Flames

I unveiled enlightenment in your naïve brown eyes
With our golden disposition, true love never dies
Our flames reborn through phoenix tears
An illuminating desire that burns for years

Celestial love, take me to another dimension
You and I, we were destined for ascension
The stars collide and the planets align
to remind us that our love is divine.

The freckles on your face are like a constellation
The warmth of your smile is my only inspiration
…and the two cosmic lovers between Venus and Mars
will shine ubiquitously within the stars.

.

Questions

The way your scent lingers on my skin after we part makes my thoughts wander to a different realm. These thoughts search for an answer. Little do these thoughts know, an answer doesn't exist on this earth but it exists in you. I live in a world within you and I fell in love with its palm trees and heartbeats. I wonder why. I contemplate this at night when I am alone. Questions. What is a question without an answer? Then I see you, and it all comes back to me: you can search the whole entire planet but you will never find an answer. Nothing is of absolute certainty on Earth. There are no facts, only opinions. You find answers in people and you find answers in the universe. Planets die, people live on. The Earth will perish, the universe is infinite. We are people trying to find our infinity in this universe. To love someone is a taste of heaven. To love someone is to feel eternal.

Your rainbow smile colors my monochromatic life, conveying every pleasant feeling ever felt in one simple action. You speak of no knowledge, you have a stuttering soul and a dyslexic touch that I can't get enough of. Somehow the two of us formed a magnificent language that only we can understand. A language of every word in the dictionary, a language of silence. On days when I feel melancholy, your tears hydrate me and your laugh serenades me. Two insignificant human beings with anxious yet curious minds, trying to find meaning. We may be just a drop in the ocean, but even the ocean envies the depth of our love. I feel higher consciousness in your arms, and if I am nothing but a body, at least I found truth inside of this world we built on our own.

Caesar

An empty chair
an empty desk
can go unnoticed

Here is my confession:
I never think of you; you never even cross my mind.
Like a grain of sand on a West Coast beach,
if you were gone, I would not enjoy the beach any less.
Yet somehow today, your absence reminds me of fate
and how that empty chair
that empty desk
could've been

me

and

no

one

would

notice

Technicolor Eyes

I want to drown in your eyes
I want to die in your ocean.

And I thought that,
just maybe,
If I died there,
I could live there
forever.

July 31, 2013

If there was even a word for how I'm feeling right now it would be enchanted. Life just threw things at me that I never thought were possible. I'm feeling feelings I thought were only used for literary purposes. I cannot even think of a reason for anything; I cannot justify my feelings and I'm completely okay with that. Absolute enchantment. New experiences and new people are coming into my life and I feel so blessed. I've been trapped in emotional solitude for so long. I have great things in my life, I always have: but it's always been the same old thing. Finally I get to free myself and showcase myself to the world. It feels lovely. I am enchanted to meet you, I am grateful you graced my life with your presence, I am happy to have everyone in my life that is currently in it. I am happy I get to be me.

13

dance with me forever;

; the seagulls kiss the sky
the ocean kisses the shore
and the moon kisses the sun
the flowers bloom and they die
but are reborn every spring.
everlasting spring, plant flowers in my heart;

mahogany bookcases, never-ending flames burning in the fireplace,
old paintings hanging from our invisible wall, the morning sun
shining from our windowpane, kissing your eyelids so gently
but only I can kiss your soul;

to awaken your senses
and free your mind of all darkness,
this sluggish body does not define you
you are a dictionary with no words
we are a storybook with no end;
I promise thee
the pouring rain roughly kisses your skin but only I can kiss your
soul;

the piano whimpers on and on
like teardrops on my face
I feel your heart travel through the stars for me;
my periwinkle dress and pearls speak of those golden smiles we
planted on our faces and let grow so gracefully they exploded like a
thousand suns;
and the Manhattan nights we once had;

one and only;
forever and always;

if you are the darkness,
I will enlighten you to a bright path
with thousands of green sunflowers
If you are the ocean, I am the shore;
you kiss me, continuously, always coming back
through every tide and every moon;

I'll be seeing you in every dark red curtain in New York;
and I'll be loving you in every Bordeaux cherry ice cream cone;
dancing through each moment–only a heartbeat of eternity;
growing
infinitely;

so dance with me,
dance with me on the clouds,
dance with me in Paris,
dance with me on Saturn's rings,
dance with me then
dance with me now
and never stop
dance with me forever;

The Last Sunset

This is the last poem I write
for you.
Your soothing voice
and the way your whole body shakes when you laugh;
it's like your shoulders are screaming for applause,
wanting the whole world to see your approval.
Your deconstructionist attitude
and your shaggy blonde hair
and your annoying John Mellancamp Pandora station.

These are things I don't care about ever seeing again–
I'll never listen to your records.
I'll never drive by your house just to see if you're in.
I'll never let my breath get caught in my throat because you turned
around to talk to me.
That's not me anymore.

I've always loved your name
and I never held your hand,
but I'm okay with that.

You were so tall, I couldn't reach you,
but you made me feel something real once.
And I thank you for that.

This is the
last sunset
and it sure is mediocre;
I found my real paradise somewhere else.

Uncertainty

advancements in science and technology
cyber thoughts, no words said
no eyes met, no hands held
blinded progress & unanswered questions

"it will help us," they said.
"it will make you happy," they said.

the labels and names
proper and precise
the research and knowledge
that can't be real.

unseen things are real
dreams&faith&hope&love

no depth or youth
wasted bodies in an earth-toned room
learning about chemical reactions between
atoms
not people.

if you are a proton, i'm an electron,
two atoms in a molecule.
and I DON'T KNOW
if that's scientifically correct or politically correct or morally correct
but I DON'T CARE.

Certainty

When I read the work of people,
I read the work of people.

When I read the work of poets,
I read the work of God.

Symptoms and Obligations

Sometimes I feel like life is a string of dental appointments.
The check-ups.
The biannual cleaning.
The cavities.
And that one time I got my wisdom teeth out.

The Novocaine doesn't numb anything.
The anesthesia doesn't change the fact you're at the dentist.

Northfield

And to us,
nothing mattered because
passion and love,
purity and authenticity,
were things they didn't have.
We were real.

71 & 3rd

The room was full with eager faces
thirsty for champagne
they will never be able to afford.

Canyon View

the metal in your heart
ticking like a clock
for 14 years and 10 months

the brick-colored arm chair
the gold cross necklace
the sea green shag carpets
the white leather couch
the mahogany coffee table full of crayons
the landline at 9043
the bills and the junk mail
the sugar wafers
the Snyder's potato chips
the Lipton red tea with no sugar, just milk

that familiar aroma
that scent I can't describe
the scent of spaghetti
and expensive makeup
and thrift stores
and nightgowns

the scent of leopard print
and Florida
and nautical sweaters
and morning talk shows

the scent of home
of happiness

and everything you gave to me
and everything I give back to you everyday
I hope you're proud.

A Poetic Subtweet

if I do not like you or do not love you,
keep your trivialities away from me.

you don't even know my favorite color
yet you use your paintbrush to project all your insecurities onto my
canvas...

until I am the same color as you:
dark, dark blue.

taking every breath became my own personal Olympics,
while you critiqued the way I exist,
too loudly for you.

I was thinking about killing myself
while you were screaming over the dust of the earth.

I would never wish anything bad upon you,
and my reasoning is simple.

I already know you're never going to experience true love, true
friendship, or true happiness.

And maybe,
just maybe,
that's why you put so much effort into trying to take mine away.

Blue Bubbles

i am aware of your intentions,
treacherous yet enticing–
pulling me in with every word, every operative glance.

i do not want anything to do with you,
yet here i am.
blushing at my phone at 1:59 a.m.,
wanting to feel your fingers on my keyboard,
losing sleep over three white dots trapped in a gray bubble.

you are the illness i will never cure,
you are the the poem i will never write,
you are the thought i will never finish,
you are the text i will never read.

i will always have the power.
but today,
you found my off switch.

23

Peach's Song

you saw my life as a video game.
it didn't matter how many times you killed me,
for my lives were unlimited.

it didn't matter how many times you hurt me,
for any potion or elixir could revive me.

it didn't matter you that you neglected me when i needed to be saved,
some other player would get to it.

at least that's what you thought.

i was only there to pass the time.
you wanted to play me until you decided you were done with me,
until something more interesting came along.
until you scratched me up enough.

you wanted to see me rot on some abandoned shelf
just so you could sell me to gamestop years later.

but i never existed for your entertainment.
so when you feel nostalgic,
put down the controller.

because i won't be on your lonely shelf,
ready to be played again.

24

Californian Conversations
(4 years later)

4 years have passed since I dreamed of this exact day–
waking up to white sheets, roses and you.

I gave up everything in my life so I could fall asleep to the stars,
but I never got to see how brightly they could shine.

Maybe I'd rather wake up to skylines instead of fairies.
Maybe I'd rather swim by myself instead of swimming with mermaids.
Maybe I'd rather do nothing at all.
Nothing at all sounds quite nice right now.

The cold sweat of guilt drowns me as gentrification follows me–
I cannot breathe, I cannot smell the roses.

You tell me I rush my way through life,
I tell you I do not have a choice.

You tell me I walk too fast,
I tell you you walk too slow.

We were walking in North Hollywood
and all I seemed to care about was what I wanted.
Was I being selfish?
That word seemed to follow me my entire life.

Every block someone wanted my attention
but I just kept walking.
They wanted my money,

they wanted my time for a survey,
they wanted me to check out their mixtape.
Every "excuse me" made me walk faster
as I continued to be desensitized to all the madness around me.
I thought that was normal–
of course, that was all I've known for the past two years.

Then, as one man was forcing his mixtape in my face as I ignored
him, he said to me, "Oh, we have a New York girl."
I brushed off the comment. In a sense he was right. New York was
the place I felt most comfortable and I've lived with a New York
state of mind my entire life. Did this mean I was passive? Did he see
that I was rushing my way through life, too? Am I a self-centered,
dead-inside, dehumanizing, career-driven New York type girl now?

I'm sorry.
I am delusional and comfortable.

I may be a pedestrian on the road but I am not a pedestrian in life.
So go ahead, run me over. Run me over until I cannot feel it anymore.
I will haunt you and love you all the same.

More Than Just A Body

i don't normally turn people into poetry mid-conversation.

but there was something about the way you said my name–
like a west coaster gone east,
jokingly dropping your voice down an octave
so you could capture the essence you imagined my past to be.

you showed me that the question shouldn't be what's in a name
but how you wear the name.

it doesn't matter that my name is maria.
because it could've easily been mary or mariah or maritza or marie
or mariella or mariam.

i would still carry the sweetness they see and the spice you see.
i would still wear the accidental side pony
you've come to appreciate.
and you would still have a waterfall of curls
spilling out the front of your hat.

go ahead, say my name again in every accent & dialect–
tell me if anything changes.

we were talking like iris murdoch & john bayley
and i told you how i felt objectified in both work & play…
just a body that corporations can make money off of.
just a body that exists solely for the pleasure of mindless men.
i felt like a catherine earnshaw or rose dewitt bukater–
a victorian woman owned by anyone and anything with money.

but you–
powered on nothing but adderall & jasmine tea,
were the only one who understood.
you saw me as a boss.

for a moment,
i was more than just a body.

that day,
you were a personified self-help book,
a kendrick song put to life.

ironically,
i didn't have to listen to you–
you were listening to me.

you told me you wanted me to write about you.
nervously, i laughed, "one day. one day."
little did you know
your body would become a statue built from my words,
as i wait at the bus stop a few blocks away.

with falsified plans and dusty numbers lost among contact lists,
you decided to let me go.
why pretend we'll keep in touch?
you left it up to chance, & i may never see you again,
& i don't think i want to.

i appreciate you for your existence, your words, and your time.

i live in a shell,
so i can't blame people when they don't want to crack me.

but people like you are the reason i left the nest.

you said my name one last time.

i smiled back at you, cinematic & uninspired.
"I'll see you when I see you."

26

Quiet, Not Blind

the ghost next to me won't wake up,
the demons in the screen won't pick up
and the ghouls that live above me beat me up.

i'll refresh my email,
again and again.
i'll refresh my words,
just to make sure i was clear.
only to find out i was nothing but spam, junk, trash.

i'd rather be unread and invisible
than read and forgotten.

i didn't know it would come to this, but this is for you:
*i'm sorry for congratulating you on your disastrous career. i'm sorry
for wishing you a happy birthday when no one else did. i'm sorry for
listening when the world silenced you. i'm sorry for writing you novels
when everyone else wrote you sentences. i'm sorry for blindly support-
ing all your choices while everyone else threw rocks at you.*

as austen said, "I AM QUIET BUT I AM NOT BLIND."
you didn't get the memo though, did you?

i'll apologize one last time:
i am truly sorry for caring. i am sorry for raining on your desert.
what do i know?
maybe you like living a dry life.

i've gone through enough world war.
i cannot be burdened by your pixelated archive of nothingness.

27

The Librarian I Used To Be

when i was a little girl,
i wanted to be a librarian–
surrounded by words on pages
and expanding brains.

then one day,
i realized i didn't want to spend my life silencing people.
shushing them, kicking them out, telling them to be quiet and looking for a reason to complain.

i love seeing people dance on public transit.
i love seeing couples fight at dinner.
i love seeing people smiling down at their phones.
i love seeing people shamelessly take selfies in public.
in a country full of civilized men and women,
it's refreshing to see people
dance, fight, scream, smile, EXPRESS.

i have no time for blandness anymore.
i keep seeing men order plain bagels with no cream cheese or toppings and i keep on thinking,
WHY? what is the point of eating something with no flavor or substance
then i realize some people eat the way they live:
blandly and flavorless, quiet and emotionless…with no depth at all.

so tell me:
what the hell was i doing?
i became the librarian of our own sanctuary,

silencing you when you wanted to sing,
making you static when wanted to be kinetic.
why would i take away your voice?

"STOP READING. START WRITING.
STOP LOOKING. START LIVING,"
i would tell you, hoping we could find ourselves again.

why was i holding onto my past,
the books i used to read,
the poets i used to love,
and the librarian i wanted to be?

after all..

i always hated how we went out of our way to go to libraries
just to pick up books we would never read.

we were not meant to read stories anymore.

we were too busy writing our own.

28

The Calm Fog

you may just know me as the girl who was hopelessly in love with
harry potter,
and i can live with that.

you were always the harry to my hermione,
flushing away my erratic anxiety
with the rudest sense of realism,
with talks of insects
and suicide
and the big bang theory.

i never played with the slugs at recess
because i didn't want anyone to know i got my hands dirty for you.

your laziness made me look fiercely productive.
and now, i could use that juxtaposition in my life more than ever.

you were the calm fog i saw on highland every morning.
i never saw what was ahead of me which caused me to be unstable–
but you made me feel okay with it all.
calm fog, lazy fog, gray fog.
making my surroundings slowly fade away.

no one liked you but i did.
i always had a thing for
tragic heroes
and astrophysicists.

you scientifically proved to me that gravity doesn't exist.

so every time my hypersensitive heart aches and i feel the weight of
one billion quarks on my chest,
i laugh and i laugh,
because it's not real.

i had the best adventures of my life killing zombies with you.

i was so deathly afraid you would spend your life alone and eventu-
ally turn into one of the zombies we killed together.

because i always loved you in such a pure way.
(but not enough to hold you.)

now i see you through a familiar lens,
smiling, with your head up, aware as ever.
and most importantly, so, so alive.

i hope you're killing stronger zombies
and discovering more universes.
i know i am.

29

Funny Girl

there is one adjective that'll ruin your life.
funny.

once someone calls you funny,
you're cursed.

no one will take you seriously anymore,
for you are their personified joke.
they'll mock your words,
find loopholes in your art,
and use you for their personal gain.

you'll never take a compliment again because you fear they'll take it
back
and you'll slowly feel worthless because people see you as their
zoloft.

once you are funny,
you cannot be anything else.
you are a joker,
an amateur comedian,
trying to break the curse someone with good intentions gave you
decades ago.

so there i was, funny.
i wouldn't call myself hilarious or witty, even.
i was a funny girl.

people ripped away anything feminine or fragile about me.

they forgot i needed love and companionship.
they pointed their fingers at me when i was on the dance floor
and i would hibernate in embarrassment for days.

when i got a new dress
or did my hair
they all competed to see who could humiliate me the most,
forgetting to realize the effort i put in.

i knew i was a funny girl,
but i also knew i was so much more than that.

i let others' words define me more than they should.
i let people i barely knew put me in a shell.

but when i went home i would write poetry
and sing sad songs about pretty girls and boys
and i felt so unpretty, so worthless
because i was so laughable.

i never thought anyone would love me because i didn't see myself as
a soulful, breathing girl.
i saw myself as an adjective.

one day i got up on stage and told them i was the greatest star.
they didn't believe me, but they still chuckled at my jokes backstage.

but i didn't care much, no, of course not.
i woke up one day and i made my bangs blunt,
because i was ready to be trenchant.
i put on a black chiffon shirt
and some red lipstick,
because i was ready to destroy the shell everyone built for me.

i remember starring into the horizontal mirror,
apprehensive and afraid to unveil my mask.

i am all things, i am not your words.
i am defined by me.
i am me
and you cannot define me.

i lost all of my friends
and i was no longer funny.

they still tell the tale about the funny girl they used to know,
and how she betrayed them for a better life.

how dare she.

30

The One Who Could've Gotten Away
But Chose To Stay

i would watch titanic at 11 years old and cry liters of tears because
even then, i think i knew.
i knew if fate stepped in and had us go our separate ways,
i would still be thinking of you at 101 years old–
married to some nice old man who couldn't keep my heart the way
you did.

i would go on with my life and so would you.
yet you would own my mind more than my 9 to 5 job, my small
town home or my two kids,
i know my life would be painfully normal without you.

i would keep you in my soul, my deep ocean of secrets,
and put you into my words.
only paper and pen would know what you did for me.

i would think about the 'remember when's every month of every year,
for the 12 young months we spent together had enough fire to energize
me for a lifetime.

but instead, we stand here now,
together, intertwined for all eternity.
my heart still goes on for you, but this time,
burns a flame bright enough for the two of us.

you read my writing and call me sweet names.
you freak out every time you see me.
you look at me like i'm a work of art.

you buy me my favorite snacks
and you love me and you take me as i am.

we used to swim in swimming pools and swing on swing sets,
pretending to be jack and rose.
"never let gooooo!" we'd say, jokingly and high-pitched.
even then, i think we knew.
if the cool tide tried to pull us apart,
we were never going to let go.

31

Black, Beige, & Blended

They say how you drink your coffee says a lot about you.

Well, I've always admired your taste buds
and your heart rate
and your tired eyes.
Open to all, ready for everything.

A palate so flexible and capricious.
You love your coffee black
and you love your coffee beige.
You just starting drinking chai lattes
and you have a soft spot for white tea.
You'll even take it blended,
drizzled in caramel and toffee nut.

I could order you the whole menu
and you'd sincerely smile through each and every honest sip.

You'll treat the barista like they're the Van Gogh of coffee–
making their long shift taste a bit sweeter.

If the way you drink your coffee says a lot about you,
it tells me this:

That you greet life like an old friend.
You smile at ducks in ponds
and latte art shaped like ducks in ponds.

You see the world as your canvas and people as individual works of art,
welcoming them into your world with zero intention.

You don't mind change and you keep your tastes versatile,
because you know the essence, the soul of things stay the same.

You love me when I have no caffeine in me
and you love me when I've had a bit too much.
After all, you know my soul, my essence, is still the same.

Coffee is coffee.
Why complicate something so simple?

32

Meal For One (For Two)

splitting a meal for one
because we could never afford two
it can get kind of empty
but i like sharing the same tastes as you

so we could talk about the spices
the thai sauce of our dreams
the lavender lemonade that actually tasted like lavender
the latte that wasn't too sweet
the pot pie you fell in love with
and the vegan buffalo wings that won us over,
we'll sing an ode to them all.

we don't care about the coordinates
the stigmas and presentation
the critics and the influencers
shouting, "you have to go here."
we've all seen it in text and heard it from their mouths.

but our taste buds can't read or hear.
as long as there is a cushioned booth in the back corner of a café
…somewhere, anywhere,
we will get a meal for one for two.

i realize not every day can be like that,
our wallets and our non-existent car would agree.

so you get the chester's
and i'll get the limon

we'll both get a steaz.
and if you're feeling up to it, we can buy grocery store avocado
sushi.

our stomachs may never overflow
but our hearts will,
in perpetuum.

Black Lives Matter

I do not feel safe,
in an America where white men can violently rape
and roam free because it's a "mistake,"
while innocent black men are left without breath
because their existence is seen as a threat.

Cough Drops and Foxes

i may be looking down,
but i know i'm with you.

you got me kombucha
and sushi
and an orange mango smoothie.
that's when i knew we were back in the game.

i'll split my screen with you if you keep your eye on the prize.
i'll even let you sleep on the grey pillow, too.

i'll buy you honey bear lattes from that place on willow street,
reminiscent of your old sea green living room,
where our ghosts used to meet.

these shades of brown, grey, and dingy white may puncture my
mood
and these superficial energies may dim my lights.

but together?

it's like driving through the cities of our past in the middle of the
night.
drowsily mumbling,
filled with gas station food,
the static hum of 105.9 playing in the background,
knowing we don't have to set an alarm for the next morning.

that's what it feels like.

cheap plaster and chipped paint and stained carpets and shitty people may destroy me.

yet no matter how hard they try,
they can't touch us.

35

Tiny Rooms

i often think about what bukowski said about the old dogs
fighting so well in tiny rooms.
crazy as ever
hitting their typewriters hard
without women or food or hope.

and i remember what started it all for me.
i wanted to burn everything–
every bridge that would bring me back to what i used to know.

i can't swim or drive or fly,
so please don't ask me to.

i can't get to you now.

while you're investing in stock,
i'm investing in fear.

i don't live well
but i live fine.

mornings are always erratic–
the mattress is on the floor and the coffee is cheap.

i don't care much for anything else.

how many tiny rooms will i sleep in?
how many tiny rooms will i write in?
how many hypothetical conversations,
existential conversations,

can i have before i'm taken seriously?
until i can feel the thrill of being alive?

i don't care much for anything else
but feeling somewhat alive
even half-alive would do.

i always crave what i can't have.
come and find me.
i'll be in a tiny room somewhere.

36

I Went Out of My Way to Taste You

i never expected you to follow me around.
now i realize it was wishful thinking to even expect us to run into
each other.

you saw me as i was,
and i saw you, too.

the skies were aurulent and honey-like.
i could appreciate it but i could never relate to it,
because i was born from lava–
bitter and astringent.

so i spent all this time retracing my steps,
trying to convince everyone i was coated with sugar,
reminiscent of cotton candy clouds and heaven–
and they believed me.

i fooled myself, too.
but their taste buds couldn't lie.

i was never sweet,
i was conglomerate.
i was nothing but the acidic coffee they couldn't drink black.
i was for their consumption–
i didn't exist for anything else but their mindless consumption.

so there i was,
getting stirred and tainted until i tasted right.

all i ask of you is:

don't follow me around, don't drink me dry.
just let my trimethylxanthine flow through your mind.

37

I Don't Want to Be Cute

i am not as sugary sweet as you think i am.
they see me in silence, observing the pedestrians.
they see my cheeks turn pink at every word.
they see my lashes bat.
they see me let them take advantage of me.
"aw, she's so cute!,"
they'll say to me.

but it's always surface.

cute cute cute.
like a mindless baby or a helpless puppy–
cute.
never beautiful nor intelligent.
never stunning nor hilarious.
never provocative or captivating
or so mind-blowingly interesting
just cute.

i may not show you all my layers and colors
because i am nothing but a lazy acquaintance–
never fond of small talk or cheap jokes.
not fond of women named jane
or men named joe.

but those layers and colors are there and i don't like them to be dis-
missed by the flatness you see.

i am not an image

or a facade
i'm not a robotic fairy
waiting to hear your virtual claps for approval
// just to simply breathe.

did you know i take each and every breath?

do you know how hard that is for me?
why does everyone see me as a sink
when i am an ocean?

don't call me cute.

it makes me feel so small.
i demand words with more letters and more meaning.
because when i am called cute,
i am being seen as empty, mindless, and unknowing.

candy and honey and sugar are not names for me.

i am a ghost pepper,
a myth to many.
but realer than most.
unapproachably, devastatingly…
real.

why can't i help but feel like everyone i talk to is downplaying my
existence?

i don't want to be cute anymore.

38

"What's Your Biggest Fear?"

i shouldn't be imagining
when i have all of this right in front of me.

and if i was doing what i was imagining
i would be imagining what i was doing now.

i would slap myself in the head for taking
all that i loved for granted and trading it for
the jittery imagery of scenery i craved.

so i listen to this fucked up playlist of emo music
and think of my deepest
darkest
fears.

usually in playful conversation
the passenger seat
will turn to me and ask,
"what's your biggest fear?"

i stare into the distance,
sighing because i'm at a loss for words.

"nothing, really. i don't know. i just can't think right now."

finally–on a night bus to nowhere i realize.

my biggest fear is not being able to hear the music.
not feeling tingly in my stomach
or not feeling such immense emotions when

that emo playlist plays
and hits my palate.

my biggest fear is becoming immune to your cancer
not being able to taste the tears of every song.

each and every cell
proton
and quark,
doing everything in their power to make sure
i don't break out in a smile when your hand touches mine.

i fear the days molding together,
without a title to define it.

i fear the symbols of nature
will soon
just be biological names
in a dictionary and i won't feel a thing.

i think i fear being numb.
i fear cynicism taking over my body
until i am drenched in frostbite.
i don't want to be immune–
i want to be so ill
if that means i get to feel something.

39

Mustard & Mint Green

So what if I write a poem about you?
I don't like you or love you.

I was wearing fourteen layers of mustard and mint green
and you briskly touched my back with your hand so lightly.

You were moving behind me,
but you didn't have to touch me.

There was so much space between my back and the wall.
I felt shivers down my spine.
Still–
you didn't have to touch me.
But you did–
so lightly.

Your hair flows like a Spanish river.
Your face straight out of a Renaissance painting.
And your skin no lighter than mahogany.

If I could put you in codes and unlock you, I would.
But I would rather just leave my window open
and listen to the robotic owls.

So it goes:
who cares if I write a poem about you?
I know I'm not worth your time.
And you certainly aren't worth mine.

For there are such beautiful and aesthetically pleasing things for you

to look at.
For there are so much more important things for me to do.

I am not beautiful,
but unfortunately,
I can't say the same for you.

40

Triforce Twilight

singing about turquoise rooms & skyway avenues
i didn't want to leave.

we were alone in a building of 32 stories
the floats were flying past our windows.
everything was ours.

i remember we woke up late,
but once we got to 58th and park,
we saw the snow fall
as the flags were waving.

that's all long gone.
and so is the poem.

unless something magical happens tonight
to save me from the blanket of sadness that covers me.
i'm too afraid to take it off,
because you told me california gets really cold in december.

i'm not thankful for many people
or places
or things.

we were drenched in vanilla twilight,
that song was always our guilty pleasure.

all i want to do is be at hogwarts with you,
eating turkey legs in the great hall
listening to the carols of the ghosts gliding past us.

then maybe we could go to hogsmeade and get a butterbeer.

i want to be in
a cold living room
with zelda playing in the background

but instead we are on different schedules
and all i want to do is sleep.

41

The Cinderella Effect

I felt so deprived.
Not of money or greed or things you can touch,
but of something so intangible
yet something so necessary.

It was I who chose freedom.
Freelancing through every concrete ceiling
and frolicking through every cultural forest.

Is there a land of the free?
Or does it cease to exist?

I am controlled by a devil,
a parasite sucking energy from within.

How can I frolic
or skip
or dance
if my metabolism burns all the fruit it gets?

It's a mental anorexia,
you can taste it in frequencies.

Living bodies from every borough and every tongue–
seeing me as a slave,
throwing their selfish demands at a girl who was an expert at invisi-
bility.

I was Cinderella,

on my hands and knees–
cleaning up messes for those who didn't care about me.

I was living to please,
with dirt on my skirt
and a song in my heart.

My best friend was a squirrel
and that's not even remotely a metaphor.

You may read this and wonder who it applies to.
Is it a general statement to society?
Is it from my personal experience?
Or perhaps is it about you,
the very one reading this?

I write to confuse the minds of those who live in zero debt of the
hand but major debt of the psyche.

However, if the shoe fits,
it fits.

42

Cruel To Everyone But You

it has always been this way.

iced green tea with hints of mint and lemongrass
remind me of you.
and it reminds me of the girl i used to be.

every orchestra and choir full of sopranos and tenors
sing the songs we used to sing,

but maybe you're a baritone now
and maybe i've always been an alto.

i still like the words you sing
and how they vibrate through the air
even if you're trying too hard.
{you're still cuter than everyone else}

you used to summon the angels with every note
and i used to cry every time you did.

when the curtains would open,
i knew one thing for certain:
my cheeks were blushing more
than each and every rose you would hold that night.

it was probably march or april or may,
but all i remember is my
long chestnut brown hair
with no tangles or tears
touching the wind for you.

i am reminded of you too often
and it feels so wrong
because you are standing right in front of me
laughing like a little kid
dancing for audiences bigger than before
yet i miss the acoustic hymns we used to sing in the small towns we
inhabited.

i don't want to write anymore
even if everyone is reading,
unless it's about you.

so i sip on that iced green tea,
trying to take mental notes
of the notes of lemongrass and mint.

i close my eyes and dream of spring.
autumn and winter may make my heart do a temporary dance,
but the spring we bloomed together makes my soul do endless
pirouettes.

43

Cable Lock

I observe from afar
with my telescope eyes.
I come to the conclusion that humans are no longer divine,
they are manmade.

With the sulfate flowing through their hair and
the silicone being force fed to every living cell.

Those aren't stars illuminating her skin
and roses aren't turning her cheeks red.

I am not looking down at you–
I am staring at you right in the eye.

Yet when I lay down and touch the earth,
I couldn't feel more insecure.

I will never bloom,
for I am not a flower.

I am a tree,
I give you oxygen but you don't appreciate me.

44

First Star to the Left

the world beat me up like the imaginative frames of literature
and the elastic words of photographs.

i grow tired as my eyes fall downward
each bag darkens
every microscopic fragment of mascara
collectively telling the world i drowned in carbon dioxide
and hydrogen
and capsaicin.

i thought it was nothing but a mere quarrel between colonies
yet i stand here,
as commander general,
wondered why i signed up for this.
wondering why i brought all these innocent people with me.

i can't turn back,
i have to fight.

if i write a novel about this war,
would that make you feel better?

i look at the mirror and laugh.
i can't run away from my tired eyes–
but at least i can win a participant award.

45

Pianos of the Past

it is in these moments by myself
i fall in love with my skin and all it's touched.

the fire from every vanilla candle,
the power within.
the chords from the pianos of the past.
the night.
the darkness of each fallen night,
the vulnerability within me,
drunk on just being alive.

willing to spill my colors onto yours,
making a beautiful mess,
making a color with no name—
a color undiscovered.

it is within these moments,
all cynicism melts.
and i exist as a poetic soul,
a moving woman,
drinking the world in a porcelain mug of green.

the jazz music was playing and i couldn't believe my eyes.
the magic of the city lights from the 30th floor,
projecting itself onto my freckles.

the stolen telephone lines of each and every ghost town
from fancy basements,

filled with sleeping bags and flashing lights,
reflecting our adolescent hearts.

the independence,
not red nor blue,
but blue and green.
reflecting its beauty onto my dark sandy hair,
hoping the moonlight will never get a chance,
because she will consume me,
naïve and wide-eyed.

the fleece below me could never comfort me like the images behind
me.
i hope every night is stunning wherever you are.
in my words, you are a legend.

this suitcase heart may visit very dimension and realm,
but will always carry you,
as cummings said.

that town never could break me,
and i hope you find your vocal range.

7-Eleven

i wasn't upset because of
the dent in my cheap car
the cracks in my outdated phone
or the slurpee all over my overpriced outfit

i was upset because i didn't care.

i don't flinch when you hit me
and i don't care for childish games.

i am numb to the sun
and i don't feel the rain.

November 4, 2012

It's Sunday morning
and nothing is enough.
I yearn for you and only you,
drowning in blankets and bubbles.
I eat flowers for breakfast.
I write.

I sleep and sleep and sleep,
yet I still have an unquenchable thirst for it.

Perhaps one day my reality
will meet my dreams.
I hope they get along.

48

The Coastline to You

the streets were dead
and my coffee was too sweet
segregating itself
like a science experiment.
but the people were bitter
and just as cold as the oceans, rivers and seas.

moments were forced
and skin was thin
melting like plastic
in the morning whim.

throughout the vagary,
i couldn't lie.
the stares and the impatience
the emptiness inside,
i was too fast,
i couldn't lie.

so forget your fake smiles
and forced conversations
forget your blind stares
and shallow consolations.

if you are the land, then i am the sea.
i don't need you, and you don't need me.

the land was too naïve,
and the water was too pure.

she proved every element wrong,
eroding all in her path
with her light, tsunami waves.

her gradual destruction
showed them all her strength
but destroyed all she loved.

but she proved them all wrong,
isn't that fucking lovely?

she was not blue,
she was not full of beauty.
but she will make it all worth it
when the world is no longer green.

where were they going?
why were they lying?
no one is an island,
we are all a sea.

if they think we are separate,
maybe they'll let us be.

Cell #15

We were always incarcerated by the cities that held us–
transferring between cell blocks,
ignorantly believing that would change our predestined mindset.

But I wasn't a Chapman or a Vause.
I was looking for something intangible to hold on to
and I wasn't going to find that in jail.

DRAÍOCHT

how naïve of me
to believe
the sun was setting for us

how silly of me
to believe
the leaves would finally fall for us

i close my eyes
for the light is too blinding
and i feel the steam on my skin
and i feel my fingers burning off with every keystroke
just as they did before,
when i was nothing but lifeless & heartless.
just as they did before.

my skin was widening & reddening
and i couldn't hide from my pixelated demons.
i couldn't hide from the truth plastered onto bricks in every borough.

it was in those vulnerable moments that i realized what i was doing.
i was spilling coffee
and tripping on sidewalks
and bumping into the walls i built for myself.

i was so afraid of you and your sharp edges.

i visit you in my dreams

and you talk to me in songs
each sentence is a bridge taking me closer
to the city that you are.

i knew each ocean would bring you to me
and i would see you on every busy street.

the tourists would stop and stare
at the blue roses growing in the middle
of the sidewalk.

they felt our telepathy
and would catch us in our silhouette dreams.
i kept on blushing
and tripping
and falling
bruising every inch of my skin just for one thrill.

the societal pressure
was falling behind
the beating of my heart
but i couldn't fight it any longer.

you're more than a person
you're an entire city.

do you know?

i'm not going to throw around more or less than three words
i cannot sugarcoat something that already has so much flavor.
i can't say much
but we both know.

for it is the draíocht that brought us together.
the childlike wonder and effortless connection
the poetic conversations between just us,

but we knew the stars aligned elsewhere.
(we can't deny it any longer.)

do you know?

my feet are in the sand and my heart resides in each and every
ocean,
wavering its way to you
holding your depth inside of it
but when i look up, i remember why you hated swimming.

and i remembered why i let go of my fear of all that's blue.
i looked in her navy arms and told her to never let me go,
because i couldn't walk on two feet
on crowded streets with you
anymore.

i'm more afraid of you now than i ever was.

51

Front and Center

Your thick-rimmed glasses
and your awkwardly zipped jacket
can't hide you from
what I know.

So take off those thick-rimmed glasses and look at me like I'm real.

I just wanted to talk to you about how Salinger is perceived wrongly
by the public and how Romeo & Juliet are actually quite clever kids.

Instead, you lived behind your stories,
slightly exaggerated with a dash of longing.

Youth lives in your soul,
not your stories.

I wish I could've told you that.
Yet somehow, I think you know.

52

My Sweater Vest Darling

Burning ashes on your coffee table from our last cigarette together.
Like a metaphor:
perhaps real,
perhaps a dream.
Always never the way it seemed.
I never smoked
and you stopped years ago
and we both know we would never do it again.
yet I would black my lungs to feel that youthful again.

My thoughts are shuffling like basement dreams,
deep down I know we were barely thirteen.

Yet I miss the thrill of your self-destructive heart
that melts in the sun like chocolate,
bittersweet and incandescent.

As much as I want to put you back in the fridge and freeze you back
to your original state,
it's too late.

You would be trapped in a wrapper
that doesn't fit the way it should.

I could open you up but would it be worth it?
Would you taste the same?
Would you still smell like smoke and rain?

I'll never know.

So I thought I would leave out all the rest,
my sweater vest darling.
You're worth a thousand cigarettes and a hundred acoustic songs.
Yet the human soul is known to find the good in things
and to feel nostalgia even when it's wrong.

So maybe I'm wrong.

And you knew you were too young to be this broken.
And you knew I would never truly be yours,
and I knew that, too.
We were too broken to be young,
my sweater vest darling.

53

I Am Me, You Are You

I'll live through my words and my pictures,
and you'll probably live there, too.
My naïve doe eyes and my imperfect porcelain skin mislead you
into thinking that I could save you from this town you call home.

But I think even you knew I would only make things worse.
Yet those seconds we spent together made a difference and you
know even I think about it years later.

You'll live through my words and my pictures,
and I'll live somewhere the skies are blue.

54

Ancient Hymn

I wish to offer the world more than just
beauty and plastic moments.
I wish to offer the world depth, conversation, poetry and wisdom.
I hope you do not deny me when I open those doors.
The doors were bounded by fake roses, because you know
I couldn't afford buying new roses every week.
Maybe I just didn't like watching something so beautiful die.

"What's in a name?" Well, what's in a glance?
Much more than you think.
(much less than you think.)

When the flowers bloom, my hair turns red
burning away winter's doom & her brittle ends.
His & her & her & him
living in a virtual world
of
nostalgic grins and late night swims.

you'll always be my ancient hymn
(you'll always be my ancient hymn)

55

Love Everlasting (2012)

I love us. I love our love. I love it all. The way I love your musky cologne and the way you love my enchanting perfume. The way you look in color. The exciting look on your face when something good happens to you. The even more exciting look on your face when something good happens to me. The vegetarian burritos and our obsession with black beans and brown rice. The laughter about absolutely nothing while lying in my bed. The memories on Acre Drive. The way you look in your golden Chevrolet. The way people perceive us, the way we really are. The love I see in your eyes every time I drown in doubt and the way you always carry me to the shore. The evening movie tickets hiding at the back of our wallets. The joy we feel when we see a large buttery popcorn tub in front of us. The monumental window in the small living room, watching us grow for years. The way we eat everything with Sriracha. The dreams we have, the ambition we have to achieve those dreams. The way your desk is like a collection of memories, like a collection of your thoughts. The way you notice when I paint my nails or get a new dress. The way you love listening to my stories. The way you loved me through my awkward, chubby phase, and the way I loved you through your awkward, chubby phase. The way you know when I'm napping and the way I know when you're at work. The way I get annoyed when you never stop singing. The drives all around town, looking for something new. The way you are incredibly patient with me through my anxiety. The places we've traveled together. The places we will travel together. The realization that love isn't always perfect, but in my eyes, our love is. The excessive amount of money we've spent on coffee and soft pretzels. The way you understand how I'm always overdramatic. The way we don't even understand how we got so close. The way you look in glasses and that navy blue polo. The walks through green forests, the transcendentalists inside of us. The deep conversations of the past, the small talk of now, the laughter of then, the silence of later. The way we are always together even when we are physically apart. The peaceful Cleveland autumn evenings, the windy Chicago summer mornings. The way we love similar aesthetics. The way you're not very smart but you speak of more wisdom than anyone I know. The way we talk in weird accents and voices more than our actual voices and simply cannot get enough of it. The times you surprised me with soup, flowers, and sweaters. The dances we have together, sentimental and silly. The way we would purposely try to make each other jealous in 6th grade. The way we are not high school sweethearts, but elementary school sweethearts. The way we've always been so comfortable around each other. The way you bring out the best, hidden parts of me. The way people and things have come and gone out of our life, yet we've always been constant. The way your eyes light up when you do something you're incredibly passionate about. The times we've performed on stage together, the times we've watched the stage together. The way I wake up every morning with hope because I know I'll get to see you. The nightly phone calls. The way we found ourselves within each other. The way we both act like shy schoolgirls around each other. The Seinfeld moments. The poems you wrote for me, the poems I wrote for you. The times you tried to be romantic but accidentally adorably messed up. The way you hate when I wear lipstick because you can't kiss me without wearing lipstick, as well. The way I can't remember how my life was before you. The way we are always thinking of each other in everything we do, the way everything reminds us of one another. The nights in watching television. The way we walk towards each other in a hallway full of people, but see only each other, smiling uncontrollably. The way we love taking photographs of our life. The way we crave Paris but didn't learn much in French class. The sense of independence we feel when we go out alone. The wanderlust we feel, the way we want to leave this town.

The days we would get away with sleepovers. The way we would feel like we were in our own little world, just us and the dark. The way we instantly gravitated towards each other when we met. The way we were best friends before we dated. The way everyone knew we would end up together like it was destined. The white sheets, the hotel rooms, the subway rides. The way we are always holding hands. The way you are afraid of ducks. The time you got on one knee with a daisy and asked if I would be with you forever. The way we can sit together in silence for hours. The way all I've ever wanted was to fall in requited love with you. The way my 11:11 wish came true. The way I knew from the moment I met you: I am nothing without you. The way time means nothing to us, even after seven years. The way we know our love is ethereal, celestial, divine, and of the Creator's design. The way we are like two flames burning as one. The way we know we are the lucky ones. The way I sense eternity in your eyes, the way you sense eternity in my eyes. The way we mirror each other, the way we are two individuals existing as one. The way we never believed in anything until we met each other. The fact that I love you, you love me, and it will always be that way for eternity. Immaculately beautiful, breathtaking, and full of infinite love. At last.

56

Marilyn's Theme

You pray to Mary, I pray to Marilyn.
She comes and goes like the night.

Her beauty is gone, she is nothing but a lonely soul.
Not strong enough to suffice, or take any form.
I ask her to haunt me.
I give her permission to take my soul.
I beg her to possess me.
She comes and goes like the night.

My eyes go wide and my body shivers
as the room grows cold.
I see a black shadow on my ceiling that never moves.
She comes and goes like the night.

I sold my soul to Hollywood, I sold my body for fame.
I wasted my mind and I wasted my youth
on a woman who would never stay.
I'm not sure if I was crazy, but Marilyn was there.
I could almost smell her perfume.
But she came, and she left, just like the night.

57

Faggot

noun
two syllables
six letters
"it's just a word,"
i try to reassure myself.

it's more than just
sexuality
it's more than just
a joke
it's more than just
an insult

it'll never be just
a word

a word you use to describe
a *hygienic* man
a *feminine* man
an *artistic* man
a *sensitive* man
a *caring* man
a *stylish* man
a *short* man
a *skinny* man
a man that doesn't fit your pathetic standards of what it means to be
a man.

when you use that six-letter noun,

you are encouraging
hyper-masculinity
violence
objectification
self-hate
you are the problem.

58

A Love Letter to My Belly

I am told to get rid of you
and though I'm not particularly attached to you,
I hold on tightly.

I've run for miles,
I've starved to death,
yet I can't seem to shake you off.

My collarbones
My hip bones
protruding out of my skin,
yet you still live.

Now,
I can't help but love you
for you are a sign of abundance.

You show the world I live.
You show the world I eat fine foods and drink exotic wine.
You show the world I would thrive in ancient times.

I am not going to limit myself for anyone's gaze any longer,
for there are far too many fruits for me to taste.

All of the judges and the juries who care enough to look me up and
down,
they don't know a thing about being a woman.

They love and hate the body parts a woman has
but not the woman all-together.

If you think my waistline defines my worth,
you are not worth my time anyways.

My curves may not have the credentials they crave
but I do not live for their gaze.

I no longer live for your gaze.

Now,
I stand as a goddess,
portraying the spirit of Venus.
I am artwork, nonetheless,
a Botticelli painting come to life.

You show the world I am no longer suffering.

59

Closing Doors

1, 2, 3
we rode the subway to west harlem
the seats were orange
just like the buttons on your coat
and i imagined my life there

4, 5, 6
we went back to midtown
the seats were blue
just like your jeans
and we knew this was the end

soft leather, long hair
i stood clear of the closing doors for you.

Eternal Youth

i erased every trace of myself left within other people,
abandoned within their cities & their picket fences.
they do not deserve me and all of my mediocrity.

so i'll put on that old floral sundress
i can't seem to throw away,
and i'll sing tracy chapman to you, again and again.

we're driving in your car
and it all comes back to me.

it was always you,
you are my eternal youth.

Special Thanks

Andrew–my twin flame
The team at Thought Catalog
Every teacher I've ever had
& every person who inspired these words.

About the Author

Maria Elena is a writer and wannabe princess living happily in her own little world in Los Angeles, California. She aims to create art from her authentic experiences and inspiration from literary movements of the past. When she's not writing, she's most likely eating a lot of carbs and staying up till 2 AM playing video games. But that's another story…

Thought Catalog, it's a website.

www.thoughtcatalog.com

Social

facebook.com/thoughtcatalog
twitter.com/thoughtcatalog
tumblr.com/thoughtcatalog
instagram.com/thoughtcatalog

Corporate

www.thought.is

www.ingramcontent.com/pod-product-compliance
Lightning Source LLC
LaVergne TN
LVHW041321080426
835513LV00008B/542